T0209026

ACCESS YOUR LIFE TODAY!

*Living life more passionately and
on purpose*

Madisson James

authorHOUSE®

AuthorHouse™
1663 Liberty Drive
Bloomington, IN 47403
www.authorhouse.com
Phone: 1 (800) 839-8640

Published by AuthorHouse 07/18/2016

ISBN: 978-1-5246-1953-4 (sc)
ISBN: 978-1-5246-1952-7 (e)

Print information available on the last page.

Any people depicted in stock imagery provided by Thinkstock are models, and such images are being used for illustrative purposes only. Certain stock imagery © Thinkstock.

This book is printed on acid-free paper.

Because of the dynamic nature of the Internet, any web addresses or links contained in this book may have changed since publication and may no longer be valid. The views expressed in this work are solely those of the author and do not necessarily reflect the views of the publisher, and the publisher hereby disclaims any responsibility for them.

CONTENTS

FOREWORD

This book surely contains life principles that are timeless and beyond value. Every one of us, formed in the image of the divine creator wants to wake up feeling charged and excited ready to perform and conquer what life brings daily. To do this is possible. Why? Because as the book reveals you have the power over your life and the direction it takes. Ask yourself "what have you done with the gifts you were endowed with"? Is the answer fully favorable to you? Regardless of your answer I invite you to turn the pages, and discover how you can step boldly, dream, be productive while taking care of your health and let excellence be your cornerstone. A book that is worth reading authored by an excellent persona...Hausa.

Immaculata Hamilton
Business Woman

The first time I met Hausa, I did not like her. She seemed frustrated at having to be in this place and she made it known to all the attendants around her. She squirmed when touched and responded vehemently when offered sustenance. From the onset of our meeting I knew we were going to have a tumultuous relationship. You see, we saw things differently-I am a doer-first-think-later and she is an analyze, think-next, analyze, think-second and teach.

Can you imagine-total opposites. Oh, by the way, she was a day old when we met and I was two years old. But age is irrelevant, character tends to show from the very beginning of a person's life and experiences will either grow your character or shrink it. But education was the direction that Hausa took and it was a surprise in the beginning when she became an educator as opposed to a pure scientist. But after reading her excerpts I understood why she became an educator. She was frustrated by the one-sided way that so-called veterans react to students in and out the class room. She decided to look beyond the grades and stereotypes and delve into to the responses that students gave when confronted with situations. To her, the responses go beyond the oral comments and answers into the truth behind the body language and the eye-rolling.

But fear not, she goes beyond the children and gets to the core of the adult discrepancies. Is the information new? Perhaps not; but that is not the point is it? She gives you a nasty truth that is take-it-or-leave-it but can-not-deny-it-fact; and that is the point.

I do not want to be a spoiler to the experience, so if you too are interested in the truth behind the body-language and the stereotypes then flip the pages and read. You may not get it the first, or even the second time and that is the point. It is a learning exercise and every time you read it, you discover something new and applicable and encouraging.

Funmilayo Carroll
Sister

INTRODUCTION

"The Price of Greatness is Responsibility."

Winston S. Churchill

"Life is Profound; either you live it or you don't"

Madisson James

You did it! Yes finally you finished the course, you stayed on line and now you're here and you're ready. You just graduated from high school, just got accepted to the college of your choice, you just got married, you just switched job environments to a new firm. You're full of excitement, you feel alive and charged and you're ready to conquer the world. You are ready to Access Your Life.

You are ready to join the ranks of the highly performing, the highly successful, and the highly accomplished in a world of great opportunity and abundance. You're ready to access your life.

Our greatest accomplishments in life are guaranteed to stimulate the best in us.

The ability to access your life and all the opportunities available to you are dependent on you and only you. If you truly believe that then you already have the greatest tool in your arsenal for your victory - your conviction.

Often times persons graduate from school with all the hopes in the world chanting well known mantras of success, joy and happiness and before long they join the ranks of the huge percentage of individuals that occupy the bell shaped curve of averagely underprivileged individuals.

Henry David Thoroeu put it most succinctly –

'Most men live lives of quiet desperation'

That was never the way that it was intended to be.

No one ever imagines that the hope and fire that so fervently drives our dreams could ever be compromised or extinguished.

And yet this is the degenerative dilemma of the human population.

We long for the unfulfilled promises of yesterday. And as time moves on, we wonder if the dream was really just that – a dream.

I want to encourage you to believe again.

It doesn't matter who you are or what you presently do, the tools that you are about to embark on in this book are factual based. Every successful person follows them and that's why they achieve the levels of accomplishment, why they serve as leaders and role models in their respective communities and why the rest of the world wants to be just like them.

If you want to wake up every day feeling alive and charged, this book has the formulas that have been tried, applied and cherished as life transformers.

If you want to understand why there is a clear distinction between the 'you' and the 'them' the latter being the average Joe and the 'them' being the individuals who have achieved the level of peace, esteem, power and comfort that are translated as nothing short of 'great success', this book is a MUST read.

If you need to know whether your identity as a person clearly aligns with the direction that you want to be headed towards in this life, PLEASE read this book.

You can't afford to waver. The fact that you opened this book and started reading means you have an aspiration for more than just living in the here and now. I believe that you want more out of life and you are willing to make an honest assessment of yourself and then adapt these critical access points to your life.

With great power comes great responsibility and to whom much is given much is required. You have the power over your life and its direction. You have been endowed with the miracle of you, an anomaly that will not soon, or ever for that matter, be repeated within your lifetime.

What will you do with all the gifts that you have been endowed with? Where will you fall on the infamous bell shaped curve? Will you move destiny in the direction of your dreams or will someone else's destiny lead you down their goal path?

I've got a question for you. Can you visualize one person whom you consider to be highly effective and successful in what they do in life? So much so that they are not only successful but they are powerful, influential bold and beautiful? This person should have a huge following of individuals and you see them as operating powerfully in their circle of influence in the world.

Great! Now throughout the discussion of the access points that I am about to introduce you to in this book, I want you to use this person as the point of reference to challenge what I have to say to you.

I think you are ready. You have what it takes. There is boldness and a hint of something spectacular that you are ready to unleash. You want something more out of life than the class of individuals that you find yourself in the company of every single day. You know that there is more to life than mediocrity and you are just crazy enough to believe that you are one of the chosen ones; a truly special and one of a kind individual.

Providence has settled on you and it's your moment to reach out and touch the hand of your destiny.

CHAPTER 1

WHY I WROTE THIS BOOK

A strong positive self image is the best possible
preparation for success.

Joyce Brothers

High school is the pinnacle of all hopeful platforms. However, some 21st century educational theorists surmise that today, the traditional school system is producing more delinquent, incapable and uncreative individuals than in any other period of time. By the time most individuals are ready to exit the traditional school system, they may be at the apex of hopeful intentions but they are not in possession of the tools or skills needed to make successful transitions.

Throughout the course of my thirteen years as a high school educator, I have always made intense observations about the types of people that I have met. It was initially astounding to find that the 'A' and 'B' Grade students and the honor roll extravaganzas were not always the ones who ended up as the great dynamos of their time. Most, certainly not all, would have had good jobs or careers, but not much more than that. That's correct; I do not particularly attribute success in life to landing a 'good' job. (There is far more to life than that). After all the scrupulous years of acquiring their great grades in school, they measured out as mediocre, joining the race of millions who got a job to pay the bills and sustain the family and maybe enjoy some leisure time here and there.

It most often than not, turned out that the students who were assessed as being average or mediocre achiever by the traditional school standard, were the individuals that ended up being dynamic leaders, awesome trend setters and the creatively motivated individuals that are admired by and followed by millions.

Now, science is not a perfect art and so of course you do have the 'perfect' student who does become the mover and shaker and the flipside is also true in many instances; average achievers do also live average lives.

However, there is no place for the average achiever in this book. That's not why we are here.

We are here to relinquish power back to you and guide you in the direction of your passion. I want to be clear right now before we go any further that success, real success, is NOT, a measure of how much money we get to deposit in our bank accounts. Success is not a comparative measure of the size and quantity of tangible possessions; there is a place for physical gratification, but it's not in the human heart.

Success in life as told by those who have attained it, is the complete embodiment of the individual who not only comes full circle with the true Purpose for which they were created but every single day of their lives is lived with power, great esteem and influence. The confidence that they have about their unique abilities is dynamic and the evidence of greatness is the constant transformation that can be viewed not only in their lives but in the lives of all that are tapped into them.

In an effort to back my findings with sound statistical data, I embarked on a journey in search of compelling data to support my conclusion that the unrecognized school achiever was actually the one to make the noticeable contributions to society. My search ended empty handed. My search turned up nothing to match with my data because the life of the student who just makes it out of high school on the 'C' pass is never the life highlighted. Statistics reflect the extremes, the 'drop out' candidates and the 'high flyer' candidates.

The perception of the average school student is unassuming; Yet my research, results and conclusion point to a story ending worth acknowledging.

The students who moved on to live awesomely and on purpose producing trails of fire behind them lived by a set of principles that weren't obvious to everyone else.

The average school system caters to a particular type of success for a particular type of individual. Its dynamics are based on the ability to take in subjective data and reproduce mostly subjective data. The individuals who are masters of this system are then one day released into a world of objective probabilities.

To be subjective is to be prejudiced, one sided or to have a skewed view or perception of your reality.

The objective individual is the one who can shape their destiny because they have unique insight and perception of their reality.

At the end of every day, it's not a job, position or career that will drive you to want to wake up another morning, to smile at the world, to be in complete fulfillment of who you are and who you were created to be. You must be continually challenging yourself to the betterment of yourself and the fulfillment of the purpose that you were created for.

The principles that will ensure that you access your life will guarantee for you more than a job or a career, they must secure for you, personal fulfillment for each moment of every day. These principles provide you the instant gratification of living your life on purpose.

So here we go. Let's look at these access points that will change your life forever when applied as intended.

I am about to share with you the keen observations that I have made over the past thirteen years. The principles that you are about to embark on have proven themselves time and time again. They are no secrets but if you are not living the life of passion and purpose right now and today, you will find these principles refreshing as I challenge you to observe life in a new light and will yourself to intentionally master the habits and principles of the highly successful.

Put yourself in the driver's seat and give yourself permission to embark on this journey.

CHAPTER 2

ACCESS POINT 1

ENGAGEMENT

WE ARE WHAT WE REPEATEDLY DO. EXCELLENCE, THEN, IS NOT AN ACT BUT A HABIT.

ARISTOTLE

In the year 2004, I was privileged to teach and engage with a group of about thirteen kids for a period of about two years. I met with them regularly during the week for courses and interacted frequently with them on the campus.

Ben and Scott were a distraction from the start. They shared a camaraderie that though amusing to them, proved to be a source of distraction on more than one occasion. Neither boy was of the class of the honor roll 'A' or 'B student but rather found themselves in the 'C' bracket.

Though these two were distracters, they had obvious differences in habits and behaviors.

Ben was sly. He often refused to look me in the face, let alone the eyes, when I addressed him. It seemed that he was always persuaded by everything. If it moved, it got his attention and he was ready to go off on every tangent. There never seemed to be any one thing that he gravitated towards. He did not move things; things moved him. Ben never seemed to be able to identify the cut off point for his antics and so was often reprimanded. He was not an independent thinker or worker as he often tried to 'burrow' answers from other students.

Scott loved attention but he never displayed disrespect. He engaged me willingly always with eye contact and cordial responses even when he was in the wrong. There was something that emanated from him. It was like a personal discipline or commitment to something that none saw or really knew about. He got along well with his peers and always seemed to have a following; but he was never following the crowd. Scott attempted his work when given but would rather take a poor grade than attempt to 'burrow' work he did not himself complete. Scott took part in sports and extracurricular activities in multiple disciplines.

Over the course of the ten years proceeding, I have had the opportunity to see both young men. Scott, I have found to be a hard working independent business owner. He has placed himself in a field that he is passionate about and is directing his future. He serves actively in his community. What I saw in Scott's eyes as I spoke with him one lovely day in the parking lot of a common food mart was the fiery gleam of determination. He had grit, he was in the thicket and his whole attitude was one of confidence and achievement.

I have since seen Ben numerous times, and though the jovial laugh and play remain with him, they are a bit hollow now and seem more of a 'filler' than a true reflection of feeling. Ben is working for a company that he says is 'so-so' but has no concise plans or thoughts for change. There is a light that arises when he recognizes me anywhere, but the flicker soon dies when we turn to go our separate ways

****

They're engaged to be married! He or she is so wonderful and so PRESENT with their expected. They cherish every moment and they give everything in the here and now of the engagement period. She looks in his eyes and sways as she sees his total commitment to her.

Everything she says and does matters and he responds to her every whim. The energy between them is alive and vibrant. You would have to be dead not to know that there is love, passion and commitment between the pair. They are engaged!

Are you engaged?

No, I don't mean for holy matrimony but the idea is succinct.

Your engagement or your presence is the ability to become fully engaged in the moment and in the NOW.

What's your energy level when you are at home or at work? How do you interact and engage with family, friends and coworkers? Can you identify the critical moments everyday that have the potential to stimulate success.

Too many people have already abandoned themselves. The light of life that should be seen in the eyes as a reflection of the passion and purpose within has already been snuffed out for many and they simply continue to drag their unfortunate corpses around.

Highly successful people develop the skill and the art of knowing when the NOW moment fully counts and they engage 100% of their time, energy and ability into that instance in time.

You MUST develop the instinct to recognize the NOW moment.

Without recognizing and being in sync with the energy of life around us, especially when the moment is critical, we miss opportunities.

It is a selfish tendency often disguised with the attitude of not caring what may happen.

These highly successful individuals are experts in their field and worth gleaming from.

'It's about taking advantage of the opportunities you have right now, and right now we're in a position where you call somebody and they're willing to pick up and take the call because they're a fan, you have to take advantage of that and have a chance to capitalize on your ideas.'

Dwayne Wade

Luck has nothing to do with it, because I have spent many, many hours, countless hours, on the court working for my one moment in time, not knowing when it would come.

Serena Williams

When Dwayne Wade, Michael Jordan, Serena Williams or any of the other greats get on the court, they are fully engaged for that instant in time because to them that is the instant that matters to the success of their life, hope and dreams.

This level of presence was instituted, not when the first big cheque was cut, but from the moment that the inspiration and desire to perfect the art of their game became their passion. Passion led to commitment and commitment led to engagement, engagement led to high productivity and high levels of success.

The NOW moment is a critical instance in time when you can stimulate growth in a desired direction.

Your boyfriend, girlfriend, wife or husband approaches you on a critical topic to them but you just got in the door from a busy day and you just want to get to bed. The topic is so urgent for your significant other that they pursue you to engage with them on it, but you don't. In an act of frustration your companion...

You can finish the story any way you can imagine. The point to note is that in the absence of engagement, an opportunity was missed for a successful outcome. On the other hand, had you engaged, made eye contact and explained the need for a few minutes rest or if you were able to extend yourself a few minutes to ensure a successful interaction, then any number of positive endings may be achieved.

I had an interesting experience several months ago when I entered into a government office to obtain some very important documents. I approached the glass door and pressed the buzzer at the entrance to alert the receptionist who hesitated, fumbled, and finally pressed the entrance button; all the while never looking up. There were several individuals sitting around looking rather despondent as they waited to be processed. I approached the counter and proceeded to engage with the receptionist. I found this to be a rather annoying challenge as she was deeply engrossed in a game of 'diamond quest' on her tablet and my words seemed to be cascading like a stream of air over her head and to the back of her. I stopped and quickly reevaluated the situation and my tone of engagement. I spoke again this time with a tone of urgency and passion. I locked eyes with hers when she looked up and refused to let go until my request was laid out. She responded instinctively by abandoning the device and processing my request. I complimented her on her jacket and thanked her for the service she was rendering. I visited the same office over a two month period and repeated my engagement tactics each time with a successful outcome.

Needless to say the receptionist was soon let go and replaced with a vibrant engaging young lady.

Think about the number of engagements that you will face from day to day with family friends and coworkers. To join the ranks of the highly successful you will need to develop and master the art of identifying the critical moments of engagement and make your presence felt. You have to fully invest in the moment and create the energy between you and the recipient. You must be fully engaged in every moment of every encounter that matters.

Learn to make eye contact, smile and listen to the needs of others. Engaging will mean extending yourself.

Critical to the art of success in the NOW moment is diagnosing the engagements that require your participation and those that will detract from your goals.

To maximize on this point you will need to critically assess your life and all your present day interactions. Do your interactions align with the goals and purpose that you have for yourself? What do you do when you first wake in the morning, what are your hobbies, who do you keep in your inner circle? Are the interactions that you will have on a daily basis necessary for you to achieve your best you or are they just 'good fillers', time wasters are enjoyable distractions. Are you a social media junkie who is slave to the whims of the detractors or are you living a life on purpose, recognizing and capitalizing on YOUR NOW moments?

The individuals who control their time and interactions are the highly productive leaders of our day.

The NOW moments are the critical defining moments of life.

Think about it from this day forward. Determine when the NOW moments are in your life and get engaged, make your presence felt and Access your life.

Action Steps for you:

Take a moment right now to think of your daily routine.

Make a list on paper of at least three important interactions that you expect to have today.

Envision the outcome that you would like to have and see yourself engaging fully in the NOW moment.

CHAPTER 3

ACCESS POINT 2

YOUR PSYCHOLOGY

POSITIVE THINKING WILL LET YOU DO EVERYTHING BETTER THAN NEGATIVE THINKING WILL.

ZIG ZIGGLAR

It was during the academic school year of 2007 that I had the opportunity to meet, teach and engage with a magnificent and exuberant group of high school students in the capacity of their science teacher. This is an especially memorable group in that the class size was rather small and the personalities were so diverse. Approximately 15% of this group fell into the high achieving Deans list individuals while the largest percentile of 75% included the 'average achievers'. Unfortunately there were also the low percentile failures averaging approximately 10% of this class volume.

The upper echelon group were the perfect adaptables. They knew and had mastered the art of producing and reproducing work as was required of them. They seldom, if ever, had any objections or cross thoughts about the manner of instruction given them or of the academic expectations. In this they were thoroughly engaged.

Now I speak to the larger group of medium achievers. Because they were not perfectly inclined towards memorizing facts and producing scholastic proofs of their intelligence and abilities, they were not recognized in this light. After all it is only fair to bear in mind that the function of the traditional schools system is to produce the best academic scholars.

But I say that the pool of talent, charm and ability that remains untapped in the medium bracket is unbelievable. The importance of attending school… a good school should never be underplayed and that is certainly not my intent here. The social environment is equally responsible for development of the character within people as the academics is to propel academic ability.

As per my research, it showed that of the 15% of individuals that were in the 'highest expectation' category, less than one third became passionate, out of the box thinkers and leaders. The remaining individuals got a good job, making a good paycheck helping someone else to fulfill their dreams while not bothering to invest in their own.

The research further indicated that of the medium achieving group, more individuals from this bracket created out of the box industries that run on passion and contribute real value to their community.

I submit to you that the individuals that went on to live fulfilling and rewarding lives in which they sought after and attained the things that they desired, were able to do so based on several consistent principles applied in their lives.

Psychology is the scientific study of the mind and behavior. Your psychology is all about how your mind operates and how that is interpreted in your behavior. Your psychology is unique and distinct; it's all about what makes you tick.

Every individual on the face of the planet has their own personal psychology. We are all individuals and all unique in our genetic coding.

Your genetic coding is the mystical sequence of amino acid bases that are found in a series of double helix columns in our body cells. These codes are specific and they give concise details about every detail of your anatomy. When you look in the mirror and see the image starring back at you, that's a reflection of the information encoded in your DNA.

Scientists theorize that 99% of human DNA is nearly identical. The regulation of our DNA in the form of what we commonly call genes, leads to the amazing differences that we observe in one another.

However we marvel at the enigma, the fact remains that each of us is unique.

The greater propensity may then be to recognize that the immense power and tenacity required to create such coding and ensure a means by which the code is successfully transferred from one generation to another is nothing short of divine.

All of the amazing factors that contribute to your uniqueness, also confirm your distinct psychology

Take a minute right now and think about three words that you would use to define yourself.

When you think of whom you are what comes to mind? Are you passionate, bold, energetic, intelligent, hardworking, environmentally conscious, caring, charismatic, brave, thoughtful, or beautiful? Are you shy, outspoken, bitter, afraid, apprehensive, bossy, creative, fickle, impulsive, or moody?

What do you say to yourself in the morning when you stare into the mirror to get ready for the day?

Do you smile at yourself? Do you praise yourself? Do you give yourself little pep talks for encouragement?

Do you visualize the day before you and think about how you want it to unfold and what you are prepared to do to ensure your success? And do you ever question why you do the things that you do?

These are great questions. I want you to start to meditate on the patterns of behavior in your life that you have, up to this point, deemed 'okay' for you to carry out.

Your pattern of behavior will help you to clarify 'YOU'. So right now when you think of the three words that you say define you, do they align with your pattern of behaviors?

High performing individuals accomplish great things in our world because they have come to understand how to use their minds to produce behaviors that are conducive to their goals and aligned with their objectives.

So now going back to your three words, do these words align with the pattern of behavior that you exhibit every day?

And does your behavior produce the results that you want to have. Are you performing at the highest level in your life? Do you wake up charged and invigorated with amazing excitement for your day? Are you influencing those around you to cheer for you and at the same time to push themselves to higher performance in their lives?

If your answer is no, then I daresay that you are not living your truth.

If you are shy but you secretly dream to be on the theatrical stage, your cognitive behavior may be hindering you from climbing your ladder.

Or if you recognize that you are a moody person who works in a constant collaborative environment with other people, but you can't seem to get to the next level in your field, you might want to question your truth.

Your truth can best be defined as the individual that you want to be to attain to your highest performing self.

So many times we miss opportunities to propel ourselves forward in our lives because we are not honest with ourselves.

I recall a particular incident with a student once that is typical of many. Dale had been exhibiting a rebellious attitude for several weeks and was showing no signs of slowing down. He would eat and drink during class, talk out of turn, and loudly, and now he was avoiding coming to homeroom. When I caught up with him, I asked him to explain his recent behavior. His response was that he did not wish to be at school, he was constantly being targeted by teachers as a troublemaker and that he was a good child and no one seemed to care or understand. He ended by saying that school was not the place he wanted to be.

Dale was not being honest about his character or how it related to his predicament.

My response to Dale was that he had the power for his life in his hands. He could walk out of school today and not look back, but that would be his decision and something that he alone would be responsible for.

Dale, like many, was just gliding through life. He had an idea of what he wanted to be but no firm commitment to ensure that his actions matched with the ideals he claimed were his.

So what is your truth and how do others really see you?

If asked again, what three words would you write down to define how others see you. What is your social identity?

If the answers you come up with satisfy the image that you socially wish for the world to have for you, then carry on.

If however, the image created in your mind by your words is grossly inadequate in their quest to define you, then perhaps you need a new slate to write on.

Almost like an innate action, we are born blaming the people around us for not creating the right environment for us or seeing to it that we had all the amenities that we desired.

15

It takes great fortitude to accept responsibility for ourselves. And the sense of ownership of self comes by understanding our unique psychology.

High performing individuals have defined their identity and they have a very concise vision of themselves.

Action steps for you:

Find a secluded and quiet spot to do some quiet and personal meditation.

Envision the future that you want for your life and the person that you need to be to live in that future.

Write down your three words (Brainstorm with many but narrow down to three. Be specific about you.)

Allow these words to henceforth define and declare your new behavior in life. Every step you take is based on fulfilling the mandate of these words

CHAPTER 4

ACCESS POINT 3

YOUR PHYSIOLOGY

*PHYSICAL FITNESS IS NOT ONLY ONE OF THE MOST IMPORTANT
KEYS TO A HEALTHY BODY; IT IS THE BASIS OF DYNAMIC AND
CREATIVE INTELLECTUAL ABILITY.*

JOHN F. KENNEDY

On a scale of one to five with one being the lowest and five being the highest, what was your level of energy when you got out of bed this morning?

Did you feel alive, energized and ready to command your day or were you on the tired and fatigued side wishing you didn't have to get up and deal with another day?

Studies in Human Physiology are aimed at better understanding how the cells, tissues and organs of the body best work together to produce and sustain the human being in optimum health.

There are two critical areas that you must master in the quest for optimum health and high performance. Endeavor to keep yourself hydrated and get the required amount of sleep that your body requires.

Water is the major constituent of your blood ensuring that important nutrients like your calcium, iron and glucose are able to move from your digestive tract to the cells and tissues where they are most needed.

On average we typically consume about 3-5 pounds of food a day. This can be anything from homemade, processed, natural or on-the-go. Foods are chemicals like everything else around us. They communicate with our body cells and will basically tell us how to feel. The amount of preservatives, fillers, seasonings, artificial steroids and hormone that we consume varies on such large scales. Even the healthiest all natural diets will include toxins that must be flushed from the body on a regular basis.

Water acts as smooth lubricant around our joints and acts as an amazing shock absorber in the brain, the eyes and also the spinal cord.

If you are a woman and pregnant, water should be your best friend. That beautiful unborn blessing is swimming around in its own pool of water; it's called the amniotic fluid.

Forget the fact that you probably won't live beyond 5 days without water, but lack of water has been associated with everything from vomiting, dizziness, heart palpitations and headaches.

Who needs any of that when you're out trying to conquer your world?

There will always be areas in health that you may feel that you are unable to control but sleep and hydration are two factors that you must do more than just keep a close watch on, you must invest in them.

There are a million and one things that you can do to increase your optimum health but even with all that, it still boils down to two important things.

You MUST keep the body hydrated and you MUST get the required amount of daily sleep.

Ask yourself daily, "Am I well rested? When was the last time I had some water?" Listen to your body's response and act accordingly.

The average individual, as we have so often heard, requires approximately six 8-ounce glasses of water a day to be properly hydrated. And I emphasize pure water, not soft drinks sodas or even juices.

I personally recommend that sodas and soft drinks be completely eliminated from the human diet. However that is the subject for another E-Book.

More that 70% of the earth is covered with water and the same is true about your body. Isn't that amazing? More than half of you is water. So don't you think that hydration may be an important factor?

The cells are the building blocks of the body and they need water to carry out their daily activities which include producing energy and distributing essential nutrients.

That means energy and brain food. Are you willing to compromise your best energy output and most favorable cognitive output? You may be doing so already if you are not committed to proper hydration.

Are you getting enough sleep? Do you arise with bags or dark circles around your eyes?

Sleep is not just important for keeping you looking facially good but there are some important points to note about the importance of your sleep.

While you are sleeping your brain is very much alive and awake processing your daily activities and consolidating experiences. Studies actually suggest that sleeping improves the human ability to learn. It enhances your creativity, sharpens your attention and reduces any signs of depression.

Getting adequate rest and sleep also helps to ensure that your stress levels are at low levels. The cells of the body need an opportunity to recuperate after the 12 to 16 hours of various activities and strain that the body is daily subjected to.

This is a relatively simple concept but it's amazing to know that most of the world is not sleeping. Reasons ranging from work to entertainment.

Highly performing individuals understand this. They keep their bodies hydrated and they get a minimum of 6-8 hours of sleep a night.

I have to add here that as passionate as I am and I encourage you to always be, do not trade your passion for your health. There may be instances when you are moving in your NOW moment and you find yourself 'in the heat of the battle'. By all means fight the good fight, and win…but when the moment is done, get some sleep. Lay your body down and rest.

Action Steps for you:

Evaluate the amount of water and sleep that you get on a daily basis.

Make a list of your daily routine activities and evaluate whether you have the level of energy, creativity and power that you desire to have.

Make a commitment to hydrate. Get a 20 oz water bottle, keep it full and keep it with you. Also think about your water access points whether there is a water station at work or along your routine path. Make a plan to succeed in this effort.

Get the recommended amount of sleep. Check your routine. If you have to cut out an hour of television or social media, do so. Realign yourself with your three defining words as often as you need to.

CHAPTER 5

ACCESS POINT 4

YOUR LIFE METER

LIFE ISN'T ABOUT FINDING YOURSELF. IT'S ABOUT CREATING YOURSELF.

GEORGE BERNARD SHAW

The Tale of two girls

They were both young, beautiful and still in school. Crystal was in the tenth grade, loud brash and never ashamed to have her voice heard or opinion expressed. She loved the company of many, and could never be ideally tied down to one group of friends. Crystal was a social bug; a job that she took seriously and one that left her with little time to actually get any authentic school work done and so to stay afloat she would often burrow and use the work of others. Crystal spent most of her time in a single parent home with her mother but often had the liberty to spend time with other family members as well.

Sherly was in the eleventh grade. She was young and proud. She kept a small network of friends but even that dwindled as the school year progressed and she became more focused on her school work. Sherly was not the 4.0 All 'A' student, but she made significant strides and maintained the average or better in scores for all her subjects. She was selected as a senior prefect that year, an accomplishment that she was extremely proud of. As our friendship developed over the years I got sneak peaks into the background of a home in which Sherly's father had separated from her mother to live in another town. Her mother made most of the sacrifices to work and put her through private school. Sherly's drive to succeed seemed to be wrapped in her desire to make her parents proud and relieve the burdens of expense on her mother in the years to come.

It came as little surprise to many in the school system to hear of the pregnancy of Crystal later in the same school year; but what caught most individuals by surprise was the pregnancy of Sherly in the same academic year.

Both girls were expelled from the school with no hopes of readmission even after delivery of their children.

How would you think that these two stories end and what are the statistics in your region?

Teenage pregnancy is a big deal in many countries but the even greater dilemma is what happens NOW?

I can only share with you the true outcomes of these lives as I observed them.

Crystal did not return immediately to school of any sort after the delivery of her baby. In the year following I was privy to glimpse her in a back yard gathering grooming the hair of what I assume to have been clients. The set up was not very elaborate and Crystal herself did not appear to have progressed in any capacity since I knew her as a high school student. I am uncertain to this day of her whereabouts, though I make it a habit to try and keep abreast with students of the past. I have no trace of her.

Shirley on the other hand was devastated over the decisions she had made and the place she presently found herself in. She was encouraged to continue moving forward in her life and make up for any lost ground. I visited her often and encouraged her to keep moving forward. I was ecstatic to receive an invitation to her graduation from the night school she had enrolled herself in.

Sherly had a beautiful baby boy. She completed her tenure in high school (night school) and began taking college courses.

Seven years later we met up. Sherly was proud to share with me that she not only had an amazingly talented and gifted son but that she was the presiding accountant over ten churches in a particular church circuit. She spoke of the many sleepless nights that she alternated between a crying baby and her studies. She cried many nights and worked hard through many days. I saw the passion in her face and heard the power in her voice...she had overcome.

She had embraced her NOW moment and she had determined her psychology. Had she not made a conscious decision for her forward progression and then stuck with it, she would not have arrived the distance along her continuum of life and purpose.

There is a life meter for each of us on the planet. The point at which we are birthed into this existence until the time we should depart. As no one could have foretold the date that we would arrive in time so to it is unlikely that anyone can declare to us the end date on our life meter. But here's what we can be certain of; life exists for us today.

If you have ever watched the movie 'Joe and the volcano' starring Tom Hanks and Meg Ryan you might remember what to me was the most captivating scene of the movie. Joe and Patricia are on the deck of her father's boat, the Tweedle Dee. It's a cozy scene. The dramatic events leading up to this moment have included Joe discovering that he had a incurable brain disease, inheriting a fortune from a strange benefactor, and accepting the grave challenge to hop into an active volcano to appease the spirits of an island deity. Joe for the first time has had his eyes opened to life around him and he was conscious.

Patricia listens to Joe's account of the unbelievable life that he now is aware of and she had this to say.

"My father says that almost the whole world is asleep. Everybody you know. Everybody you see. Everybody you talk to. He says that only a few people are awake and they live in a state of constant total amazement."

What would that be like, To live in a state of total constant amazement?

To be in a state of total amazement demands that we are conscious of the obvious, that we are aware of the significance of each instant in time. But there's a very real enemy that sneaks in and robs us. It's fear. In exchange for a life of Adventure we settle for mediocrity because of fear. Fear of failure, fear of standing out, fear of missing the mark, fear of being called out, fear of being exposed...and rejected.

Our self esteem as the well known mustard seed lays dormant inside many of us; protected and shielded from the elements. We guard against its erosion and ensure that it lives but never thrives...just enough for one more day.

Sherly was exposed. It's difficult to hide a protruding abdomen. She was looked down on by her peers. Her teachers and the administrative staff turned their backs and labeled her as a statistic. Her decision to pursue her education meant that she had to leave the house and the neighborhood each day to attend classes. She had to open her mouth and speak to other teens and adults and express her opinions. She had to fight and believe for herself amidst the stares and expressions.

But sherly conquered. She graduated valedictorian of her class and received numerous other awards.

Sherly didn't walk the straight line but when life happened she picked herself up and made a path for herself where there was none.

What have you come through during the course of your life and how has it inspired you?

Action Steps for you:

Create a real timeline of your life. Outline all of the activities, events and dreams you ever wanted to live out and today you are still waiting to embark on.

Assess where you are right now on your life meter timeline

Make an honest list of all the reasons why you have not moved forward in your life up to this point.

Write a counter statement/solution to overcoming each reason you have listed and set a date for each accomplishment.

CHAPTER 6

ACCESS POINT 5

PRODUCTIVITY

PRODUCTIVITY IS NEVER AN ACCIDENT. IT IS ALWAYS THE RESULT OF A COMMITMENT TO EXCELLENCE, INTELLIGENT PLANNING, AND FOCUSED ACTIVITY.

PAUL J. MEJER

Simply put, highly performing individuals Produce!

You've heard the phrase 'making a list and checking it twice'. Just how important is that list?

The list makes the difference between productivity and the lack of it.

By productivity and producing I am referring to getting things done relative to what you need done in your life.

So you recognize that you are ready to access your life and you have a direction in mind. You have considered your personal physiology and you have your defining words that clearly align with your perceived identity. Now you need to make your list.

Your list will embrace the necessary actions needed for you to move from the point that you presently find yourself in to the place where you see yourself at the end of destiny's path. You don't need to be able to fill in all the tiny gaps you just need to have a list that is meaningful to you.

Depending on your position on the continuum of your life's destiny, your list can span a period of weeks to months to years.

If, let's say, your vision is to change the face of education for the nation to produce skilled workers and reduce crime then you have to see yourself in the necessary position and write your list-path to accomplishment.

Your passion in life should coincide with your vision. You may love working with children or young people and so your access point may be through education. Your list-path may look something like this:

Obtain degree in secondary education with emphasis on leadership.

Enter teaching profession and move through ranks. Teacher-department head-principal

Attain additional education if necessary. Join community education outreach organizations.

Assess the educational and social needs in communities in your country.

Join national governing body for education.

Move through ranks to obtain most influential position. Eg. Minister for education, Director of education, Superintendent of education, National President etc.

Find mentors along the way and glean from them.

This is just one of many possible paths for the goal. However the path is not clear cut and so there will be experiences, and challenges along the way, detours and even promotional events that may warrant skipping steps.

If you start with the overall list-path which connects your passion with your life goal, then you can begin to look at each step as an individual list and begin to formulate that path.

If following step one, you will need to consider schools that can provide you the combination of education studies along with leadership studies. You may want to consider other avenues for leadership training and so you will need to consider carefully how the details will work for you. This is a sub-list and may take up to five years of your life. But that's great because every day in your life is to be lived on purpose and with passionate intent.

I have often been amazed by students interested in careers in medicine who express a dread for the length of time it would require for the course of study. After a brief laugh I question them about their choice of study. After expressing their great passion to save the world from infectious diseases or reduce infant mortality rate I smile and remind them that every day of their lives and their study is a day to be lived with great expectation and passion because every day of class, and every lab session is a part of that great destiny that they have imagined for themselves.

Productivity requires that you give yourself something that excites you every morning when you wake up.

Prepare for each day by writing a list. Even the task of going to the grocery store or getting a haircut, are not menial. Creating daily and weekly lists ensures that you remain on a consistent path of productivity in the direction of your goals.

You can now ably weed out distractions and useless fillers. With only so many hours in a day and your commitment to 6-8 hours of sleep every night, listing will help you to maintain yourself on your continuum.

Action steps for you:

Beware of distractions that reduce your productivity. As simple as checking your email can be a major distraction against your productivity. Unless you are checking on mail that will actually implore you in the direction of your goals, beware of emailing and social media streams that center around other people's lives.

Block time on your schedule each day to ensure that your time allocation matches the important tasks- school related, work related or personal project related.

The habit of writing and following your list will help to keep you focused on the things that are truly important.

CHAPTER 7

ACCESS POINT 6

YOUR PURPOSE

EVERY GREAT DREAM BEGINS WITH A DREAMER. ALWAYS REMEMBER THAT YOU HAVE WITHIN YOU, THE STRENGTH, THE PATIENCE AND THE PASSION TO REACH FOR THE STARS TO CHANGE THE WORLD.

HARRIET TUBMAN

Finally, the last point to consider.

This point is the foundation on which all other points reside and can even be considered point number one.

I elaborate on this point here though we have mentioned it all through this very nice concise book on Accessing your life.

If you have come this far then I know that your mind and your heart are already on the quest and you can relate to everything that has been said so far.

The last point to consider is purpose.

Every human cell (except red blood cells) contain 23 chromosomes which contain Deoxy ribonucleic acid- or DNA. This DNA is a concise code and script for the reproduction and maintenance of the human.

This DNA is so concise that all human DNA is said to be 99% identical however, it is the regulation of the components of this DNA that produces variation.

So DNA says that we are human, and that is a grand statement. The ability to think, reason and act are based on conscious thought. The power to feel, to inspire and be inspired is astounding. It means that we are not satisfied merely by physical gratification.

The American psychologist Abraham Harold Maslow believed that people were motivated by conscious desires rather than the lure of a reward as is the case with experimental lab rats. He believed that people are motivated to fulfill their basic needs and as a need is met, they are motivated to reach for the next level. Our basic needs include food and the need for rest. After that we need shelter.

It is evident that man was created with the innate desire to progress. Fulfilling the basic need of food, water and rest ensure that the human framework can sustain itself if only to limp from one location to the next. The human is designed for survival; but then so much more.

Maslow's hierarchy goes on to include the next levels of need to be love and belonging, esteem needs and finally self actualization.

Self actualization is an intriguing concept. Maslow defines it as the point where an individual has developed the self esteem to propel them into advancing themselves to becoming the best possible human being. Here is the desire for success on a grand scale.

I think of many examples of individuals that I would pull into this case study to exemplify a profound point about the power of passion and purpose.

Booker T. Washington is a dynamic African American hero who lived from about 1856 to 1915. The fact that he was the amazing founder of the Tuskegee University in Tuskegee Alabama says nothing about the complex facts of his life that led him to such an accomplishment.

Booker T. Washington was born in the lowliest of circumstances; picture a log cabin about fourteen by sixteen square feet with holes for windows and a dirt floor.

Booker T. endured nothing less than starvation on multiple occasions. He opted to walk miles upon miles on numerous occasions on the hope of attaining any kind of knowledge through an education.

This man was so exceptional for believing in free education for the liberation of all black people. In a time when the challenges faced where not limited to physical chains of slavery but more so the shackled mindset of an enslaved people and a world in which the idea of a free educated black man was just short of a myth.

Today the Tuskegee Institute is an independent institution of higher learning. The academic programs are organized into two schools and five colleges. There are more than 3000 students enrolled and the estimated value of all assets is well over 500 million dollars.

This was burning passion that even today continues to change and transform lives.

I try in instances like these to find the correlation with philosophical regiments and humans needing to fulfill base needs before ascending the ladder to self actualization.

Again it's amazing that the most powerful stories of success come from individuals with remarkable backgrounds that speak, not to achieving greatness as a result of having completed the would be rungs of hierarchy of perceived human needs but rather by bypassing all channels to attain the high prize.

The highly successful are constantly hungry, often deprived of a support system outside of their dead-lock intense will and desire for achievement. Physical food, shelter and even companionship are not visualized as important milestones and to great extent are neglected by these individuals. There is a powerful understanding that acquiring basic needs on a temporary basis is ultimately unfulfilling and unrewarding and they opt to go straight ahead for the grand prize.

The highly successful opt to believe in themselves now rather than later. They opt for respecting themselves and others when it may not seem opportune or necessary. They have great spontaneity, creativity and a drive to get the thing done

That's purpose!

We live in a world that has been specifically designed and crafted for human life to exist. Not only is the human mind designed for creating, blueprinting and executing, but the natural world supports and engages humanity.

The trees provide beautiful scenery, food and oxygen for us to breathe in.

Gravity sustains us on the face of the earth; It's amazing that we remain rooted and grounded to the surface of a ball spinning in space at a speed of nearly 1000 miles per hour.

Our earth atmosphere is made up of 78% of an un-reactive nitrogen gas; the remaining gases are just enough to support reactivity when prompted.

That's purpose!

You woke up this morning.

That's purpose!

And inside of you, whether you have discovered it fully or you are still trying to get a grip on it and fully express it, you have purpose.

The great task of all our human lives is to understand for what purpose we were specifically created.

Purpose is connected to meaning in life and why we do what we do.

If you are still trying to understand your purpose for your life then there is one question to ask that will invariably direct you.

What inspires you?

What is that one thing that you have always wanted to be or do? From the time that you were a child there was something that made you smile, made you happy, and made you want to see the next day so that you can revel in it all over again.

Did you like flying kites or airplanes, did you love to play school, did you like swimming or playing in water, did you have a passion for food? Perhaps you liked playing doctor and the idea of healing sickness, maybe you liked digging for things or playing sports.

Whatever that thing was or is, it's probably got your purpose wrapped up in it.

Your passion is greater than a job. And fulfillment in life requires that you continue to pursue. The road never ends because purpose is not a destination!

If you could identify that thing, you can change your life today by accessing your life through your passion.

Take your passion and use it as the driving force to apply the principles outlined in this book.

Action Steps for you:

Complete each statement below with your personal thoughts or experience. Try going with what first comes to mind.

As a child, I always wanted to be a _____

The one thing I could do all day long even without pay is

_____

If I could do anything in the world I would

_____

The one thing that keeps me from acting today is

_____

The one thing I am afraid to do but I know I need to do is

_____

CHAPTER 8

THE FINAL COMMISSION

HOW CAN I SERVE MASSIVELY?

1 peter 4:10

As each has received a gift, use it to serve one another, as good stewards of God's varied grace

Service changes the world.

William's future in law as anticipated by his parents never materialized. Instead he took up a passionate interest in programming and computers that would transform the scope of the world.

It's not really the intriguing rumor about Mr. Gates never completing Harvard but instead leaving college to start a company of his own that gets me. Rather it's the fact that Mr. Gates had been fooling around with computers and feeding his fascination since he was about 13 years of age.

Wow! That's passion. Today Mr. Gates life is enthralled in the Bill and Melinda Gates foundation that services many nations around the world in providing healthcare, education and work opportunities.

With a net worth of over 70 billion dollars, I think he could afford to dedicate his life to such efforts, don't you?

Nelson Mandella could have at any time given in to his oppressors and earned a release from prison. Wouldn't the world have understood based on the tremendous sacrifices that he had already made for the fight against apartheid in South Africa? And yet…he lived his truth and reveled in his passionate belief in freedom for a Nation, and not just for himself.

Les Brown, Zig Zigglar, Earl Nightingale and others have used their remarkable talents as motivation experts to propel hundreds of thousands of lives in the forward direction. Their tremendous insight, wealth of experience and willingness to help others has helped make our world a better place.

What of Whitney Houston, Gerald Levert, Nat King Cole, Michael Jackson, Paul Mcartney, Aretha Franklin? Their voices served our need for comfort, soothing, love and passion. They delivered and with their time and wealth they served in communities at home and some globally.

And what about the foundations established by the world's giving athletes. The Michael Phelps Foundation fosters wellness and fitness in children. The Jay Cutler foundation focuses on diabetes awareness. The Shannon Miller foundation aims to fight childhood obesity. The Wade's World Foundation provides support to community based organizations that promote education, health and social skills. The LeBron James family Foundation is on a mission to positively affect the lives of people through educational initiatives. The volumes of books of good works by dedicated and inspired individuals could fill libraries worldwide.

At the helm of all great works I pause for one in particular. The most remarkable piece of work to date, in my estimation, written by over 40 authors, and over a span of more than 1000 years, foretells and depicts the life of The man Jesus Christ. More than 2000 years later, the life, mission, acts and death of this one individual, the son of God, continues to save and enlighten the hearts and minds of millions. It's not just about a life, but about the mandate of service to humanity that has rippled in the lives of millions generation after generation. That's passion and that's purpose.

What's your inspiration and how will you use it to serve?

Our purpose is in our spiritual connection. I do not speak or allude to a mystical or mythical something that may be somewhere out there in the way and beyond. On the contrary, I speak of a specific divine force present in the lives of all who would acknowledge and accept this truth.

The God that created the universe and each of us is MASSIVE. Could a comparison be made, we would stand as specks of sand beside HIM. Knowledge of this kind of truth creates the only kind of perspective that can connect you with the TRUE purpose and reason for existence.

When you discover your purpose and act on it and through it, it will inspire the lives of others.

This is the greatest part of purpose. We are invariably created to live amongst a network of individuals and with the advent of the internet and World Wide Web; your network can be your neighborhood, your continent or your world. It's up to you. But you expand your purpose and your aim for greatness when you enlarge the network of individuals that you can touch and impact through the power of your purpose.

Don't be afraid to be on the recipient end of purpose. Your life is invariably tied up in the life of other specific individuals in the capacity of your mentors.

Who are the positive, good willed individuals who you allow to tap into your life and form a part of your inner circle?

One of the greatest marks of success is humility. We all have to admit that we don't know everything and we certainly don't know what we don't know.

Trust others that have gone the path. Listen to others who have the success in the areas that interest you and don't stick to one genre of individuals. The areas in our lives that we need help with are multifaceted. Success is a people business and so we must be engaged with our mentors at different levels to ensure maximum progress and immense success in our relationships with others.

Join organizations that are invested in your interests and whom you can glean from. Serve humbly while learning from the best minds involved.

In all the things that we engage with during our lives, it s true that the best and most rewarding feeling is that of giving back to whichever cause, with no intentions for any gain whatsoever, but rather simply to help our fellow human beings to rise up from their present level.

The individuals in all of history who are known for their remarkable acts, ideas and inventions are those who discovered answers or solutions to a problem or problems faced by many.

The more people you can help the more valuable you become and the more influential. In this day and age in which we live there just seems to be so many issues. This speaks prime opportunity for the wise and willing. Solve a problem that plagues many using your gift and watch the doors swing wide open in your favor.

It is the creator's purpose and design that we abandon all vain distractions, pursue the best life, which is the one lived on purpose, and transform the lives of as many as possible.

Find your purpose today and ask yourself, How Can I Serve massively?

OTHER BOOKS AND PROJECTS
BY MADISSON JAMES

Upcoming E-BOOK, HEADS OR TAILS

'PASSIONATE PLANNERS' - 3 WEEK SERIES

'FIGHT OR FLIGHT' - 2 WEEK SERIES

'THE CHAMPION'- A TEN DAY DEVOTIONAL SERIES

ONE LAST THING

SHARE

It has been a great privilege to be able to reach out and share with you. My single goal is to reach a mass of one million with a message that CAN positively change the lives of so many hurting and doubting individuals.

If you have enjoyed this book, I would really love if you would leave me a comment on facebook or my website accessyourlifetoday.com.

Thanks.

Printed in the United States
By Bookmasters